The Felix Burns Primer

A selection of easier pieces by Felix Burns (1863-1920)

(LEAD SHEET/ACCORDION EDITION)

Selected and edited by Kim Tame

Cover graphic: Felix Burns, date unknown.
Printed by kind permission of Cumbria Image Bank, Carlisle Library

A selection of music composed by Felix Burns
From the editor's collection

Copyright Kim Tame ©2023

All rights reserved

The Felix Burns Primer

A selection of easier pieces from the pen of Felix Burns (1863-1920)

Selected and edited by Kim Tame

CONTENTS

The Blue Bird—Waltz	4
Bill Sykes—Clog Dance	5
Diana's Daughters—Waltz	6
En Fête March	8
The Granite City—Highland Schottische	9
The Great Harry Hornpipe	10
Gallant Montrose Schottische	11
The Green Park	12
Lighterman Jim	13
The Little Lift Girl	14
Maid of Devon	16
March in C: The Marlborough	18
Military Review	19
Off to the Ball	20
Song of the Seashell	21
Stirling Castle	22
Swedish Dances	23
Woodland Flowers	24
Un Chant D'Amour	26
Biography of Felix Burns—how to order	27

© 2023 The Sheet Music Stack

The Blue Bird

Waltz Cotillon from the Gaiety Dance Album

Bill Sykes

Clog dance from the Dickens Dance Album, 1922

At age 16, Felix Burns was the pianist for Zealandia, a travelling diorama show directed, at various times, by George Lingard, Sydney Colville and R.D. Paterson. This was a moving picture show before the age of cinema; pictures painted on finely woven canvas were moved on huge rollers. Mechanical and lighting effects gave the impression of movement, and there were sound effects, music and a dramatic lecture, producing, in effect, a travel documentary. The show, funded by the New Zealand government, intended to encourage emigration.

© 2023 The Sheet Music Stack

Diana's daughters

Waltz Cotillon from the Vaudeville Dance Album, 1914

En Fête March

Published 1895 in a series called Wayside Flowers, by Patey & Willis

The Granite City

Highland Schottische from the Flag of Empire Dance Album, 1916
The Granite City is a nickname for Edinburgh

The Great Harry

Hornpipe from Tower of London Dance Album, 1921. The Great Harry was a ship of Henry VIII's fleet—or a London pub

Gallant Montrose

Schottische from the Gaiety Dance Album, 1918. The title might refer to RAF Montrose, Angus, Scotland.

The Green Park

Saunter or fox trot from the Frivolity Dance Album, 1923

Lighterman Jim

Hornpipe from Black and White Dance Album, 1922. The title refers to boatmen of the Thames who ferried goods from larger vessels to the docks

Photograph of Felix Burns as printed in the *Musical Home Journal.* This was a weekly periodical aimed at the home pianist. Each issue contained a number of pieces of sheet music suitable for the not-too-advanced player, along with articles and advertisements. Felix contributed several pieces between 1905 and 1907, under his own name and under the pseudonym of Claude Rosalind.

© 2015 The Sheet Music Stack

The Little Lift Girl

Waltz from Vanity Fair Dance Album, 1915

Felix Burns published 16 dance albums between 1905 and 1923; the Royal, Imperial, Greater Britain, Flag of Empire, Royal Standard, Harlequinade, Vaudeville, Vanity Fair, London Town, Merry Makers, Gaiety, Old Drury, Black and White, Tower of London, Dickens and Frivolity Dance Albums.

Each contained the music to present an evening's dance programme, and typically contained an opening waltz, followed by polkas, barn dances, Schottisches, Lancers, Quadrilles, and military two-steps. Sir Roger de Coverley would signal that the evening was coming to a close, and that would be followed by God Save The King. The entire programme was included in one lightweight booklet, meaning that the musicians did not have to find any additional music.

Maid of Devon

Waltz from Merry-Makers Dance Album, 1917

March in C: The Marlborough

An easy march, popular with young bands, from 1895

Military Review

*Published in the Musical Home Journal, 22 November 1905,
under the name of Claude Rosalind.*

D.C. al Fine

Off to the ball

Published in the Musical Home Journal, 6 February 1907

Song of the Seashell

Published in the Musical Home Journal, 25 June 1907

D.C. al Fine

Stirling Castle

Highland Schottische from Greater Britain Dance Album, 1910

Swedish Dances

Ten of Felix Burns' 16 dance albums, published between 1905 and 1923, included a Swedish dance. The version above is the more recent, appearing in the Black and White and Tower of London Dance Albums; parts A and B of the version below appear in the Dickens, Gaiety, Frivolity, Imperial, Old Drury, Merry-Makers, and Vaudeville dance albums; part C appears only in Vanity Fair.

© 2015 The Sheet Music Stack

Woodland Flowers

Felix's personal favourite—and his best-selling piece

In an interview with the periodical *Musical Opinion*, in November 1897, Felix said that he had found it difficult to find publishers willing to accept his more elaborate pieces; his most lucrative line of work was in producing dance music and easier pieces for students and young bands. As with most musicians and composers for whom working for a living is a necessity, he had to keep a close eye on what was commercially viable.

His two best-selling pieces are included in this book; *Un Chant D'Amour* is a light piece in 3/4 time, published around 1889. The other, a Schottische entitled *Woodland Flowers*, also published under the title *Flowers of the Forest,* was Felix's own personal favourite, and perhaps his best known piece. It was printed in more than 70 editions, from 1892.

© 2023 The Sheet Music Stack

Un Chant D'Amour

Published around 1889, with a dedication to Miss Hope Temple, the Irish composer and song writer

Discover more about Felix Burns and his life in the biography by Kim Tame.

Read the story of a father's mental health issues and the family struggles that led 16-year-old Felix to join a travelling show. He did everything at a young age; he married his cousin Catherine (Kate) at the age of 19, and in his 20s settled down to the life of a working musician, husband and father in Carlisle, Cumberland. Felix's many roles included band leader to several bands, church organist, choir director, performer and composer. Not least, he was husband to Kate and father to 13 children, many of whom were also gifted musicians and entertainers.

The family had their share of tragedies; including the sad loss of four of their children at a young age, and the challenges of living through two major conflicts—the Second Anglo-Boer War and the Great War. During these times, Felix was part of the efforts to boost morale, and provide entertainment for troops and munitions workers.

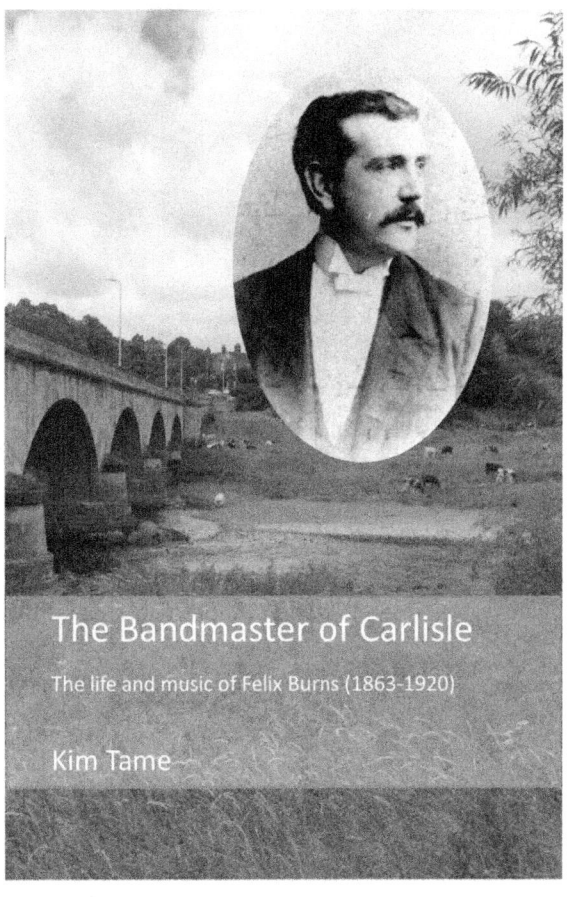

The Bandmaster of Carlisle; The life and music of Felix Burns (1863-1920)

available from Amazon, Kobo or

https://kimtamewrites.co.uk

For sheet music to download, including the largest Felix Burns collection on the web, visit

https://sheetmusicstack.com

© 2023 The Sheet Music Stack

Printed in Great Britain
by Amazon